Somehow We Manage: Two Shrinks Analyze the TV Show The Office

By Joe Guse & Luke Fairless

With Illustrations by Luke Fairless

Table of Contents

Let's Get it Started

We'd like to start by giving a special thanks to 1st Lt. Margaret Seymour of the United States Marine Corps. She worked as both a consultant and editor of our book. It was her master literary skills and diligence that helped us get this thing out in a timely manner.

Joe and I had a lot of fun writing this book, almost as much fun as we have had over the last several years watching *The Office.* We decided to add sketches to the book to provide you with both literal and figurative images of the characters.

We hope you spend as much time discussing the book with friends, debating with coworkers, and blogging about it on the internet as we have spent writing it. Writing a book is an arduous task, but knowing that others will be reading it with enjoyment makes every minute worthwhile.

Introduction

As psychotherapists who have been practicing for several years, it has become an almost unconscious habit to analyze fictional characters as we're watching them. I was a nut for *The Sopranos*, which was the first show I ever watched that made a real attempt to examine what goes on in a therapy session. I found myself going to online forums and discussing and analyzing the characters with other students and therapists, and pretty soon I became a little hooked on the idea.

With that in mind, we began to think about our favorite comedy on TV, *The Office,* which had been a faithful companion that has kept us laughing through the rigors of graduate school, and a number of other personal struggles over the last decade. The characters became a kind of surrogate family for us, and soon we were totally absorbed in their trials and tribulations like overly concerned uncles.

One day it occurred to us that perhaps the reason the show and the characters appealed to us so much was that they were every bit as dysfunctional as our own families. As we began to dig a little deeper, we discovered that some of these people had some very real diagnosable personality traits that might make for an interesting analysis.

And thus this book was born. Although we have actually thought long and hard about the various diagnoses these characters may have, it should be noted that this is written primarily in the spirit of fun. You may find yourself disagreeing with some of these opinions and determinations in this book, and that's perfectly okay. We enjoy healthy debate as much as the next guys and whose with any serious disagreements should keep in mind that there is nothing official or binding about any of this. These are, of course, fictional characters who we have never met in person.

Now with the disclaimers aside, we have tried to present arguments that support the diagnoses in all of these cases. This show is a wonderful demonstration of a number of different kinds of psychopathology, and diving into this exercise was both challenging as well as quite enjoyable. Much like dysfunctional family members, despite their faults, we love them anyway.

Included in each of these analyses will be a five axis DSM diagnostic workup. For those familiar with psychological jargon, this needs no further explanation. For the other 99 percent of you, this needs a little clarification.

Axis I refers to clinical disorders, including major mental disorders, and learning disorders. Common Axis I disorders include depression, anxiety disorders, bipolar disorder, ADHD, autism spectrum disorders, anorexia nervosa, bulimia nervosa, and schizophrenia. These are the diagnoses primarily used by clinicians to make their primary diagnosis.

Axis II includes personality disorders and intellectual disabilities. Specifically, the personality disorders include paranoid personality disorder, schizoid personality disorder, schizotypal personality disorder, borderline personality disorder, antisocial personality disorder, narcissistic personality disorder, histrionic personality disorder, avoidant personality disorder, dependent personality disorder, and obsessive-compulsive personality disorder. The existence and treatment of personality disorders are controversial topics, and most clinicians are reluctant to use these in their clinical work, as it is often very difficult to get reimbursed by an insurance company when using one of these as a primary diagnosis. They are, however, used in this book as some of the characters certainly appear to meet criteria.

Axis III includes acute medical conditions and physical disorders. This is where any health related issues would be placed to help future clinicians understand the physical challenges a client might be facing. Axis IV: refers to psychosocial and environmental factors contributing to the disorder. This is where a clinician would list challenges a client might be facing in their everyday environments. Common listings here might be problems with primary support group, financial problems, as well as issues someone might be having with school or in their jobs.

Finally, Axis V refers to Global Assessment of Functioning, shortened to "GAF" for the purposes of diagnostic discussion. This axis has two scores, one of which refers to a person's current functioning, and one to their highest level of functioning in the last year. This scale goes from 1-100, with 100 being the highest state of functioning. For reference,, a person with a score of 75 would be a highly-functioning person, whereas someone with a score of 50 would be someone in need of immediate clinical intervention.

Creed Bratton

In an office full of colorful and even bizarre characters, none can hold a torch to Creed Bratton, whose cryptic comments and delusional behavior often indicate that he has had a fairly significant break with reality. Creed's background is a mystery to the viewers, although bits and pieces are revealed through his often strange and even shocking revelations during the short interview clips the series provides. In assessing these clips, we find that Creed has worn a number of hats throughout his lifetime, and sorting the truth from reality in these cases always adds to the enigma that is Creed. Diagnostically we have a number of possibilities to consider here. Is Creed delusional? Brain-damaged in some way? A full-blown sociopath? Ultimately it is up to the viewers to decide what they want to believe, but we are given some clues that at least some of what Creed discusses in his monologues actually appear to be true.

In formulating a psychological workup for Creed, it is useful to start at the beginning, although it is difficult to pinpoint exactly what is and isn't true from his various references to his early life. We are told that Creed was not raised by his natural parents, as he informs the viewers in a webisode that, "I was left on a doorstep and adopted by a Chinese family. That's why I speak Chinese. They bound my feet because they thought it would make me more attractive to prospective suitors. Unfortunately, they realized later that you only do that to women. I lost a toe because of that." Although this story seems on the surface to be absurd, the idea of Creed's missing toe again resurfaces in "Take Your Daughter to Work Day," when he terrifies a group of children by offering to show them his four toes. Lending further credence to the story of his origin is his ability to speak fluent Mandarin Chinese, a talent he displays early on in the episode "Dwight's Speech."

One thing that becomes clear through Creed's various monologues, is that he was highly active during the 1960s. It is important to note that there is a strange fourth wall dynamic going on with Creed, as his name on the show, Creed Bratton, is the same as the actor portraying him. The actual Creed Bratton was a fairly famous base player in the band *The Grass Roots*, who had a big hit with the song "Live for Today" in 1967. Blurring the lines between reality, Creed discusses in the episode "Booze Cruise" how he was a member of the band in the sixties,, and in a deleted scene discusses how he continues to use drugs he used in that era, that marijuana was his drug of choice, and that his prolonged use of various drugs has left him "unable to concentrate for more than 90 seconds." He demonstrates his musical ability in the episode "Booze Cruise," where his guitar playing delights and astounds the people aboard the ship.

Beyond his musical career, we also are told by Creed himself in the episode "Fun Run" that he was "involved in several cults" and he further leads the audience to believe he was both a leader and a member at various times throughout his life. We are also reminded of Creed's highly exploitive nature in this episode, as he explains that "you get paid more for being a leader," suggesting he most likely bilked members of his cult out of their money. We are reminded again and again throughout the series of Creed's exploitive nature, but are also reminded that he hasn't always gotten away with all of his schemes. Specifically in a deleted scene from the episode "The Convict," we are told that Creed spent time in prison, where he made his own wine in the toilet, which he thinks back on fondly as demonstrated by his comment, "God I miss that stuff."

We are given actual proof of Creed's criminal behavior in the episode "Cocktails," when a number of young-looking people are drawn to Creed in the bar, shaking his hand and greeting him as a kind of hero. When asked by the documentary crew to explain this dynamic, Creed discussed the fake ID business he runs out of a trunk with equipment he stole from the sheriff's office. We also have evidence that theft is a consistent part of his criminal repertoire, as demonstrated by his behavior in the episode "Casino Night," where he spends the entire evening stealing people's chips, and is quoted as saying, "I love stealing things," and "I steal things all the time. It's just something I do. I stopped caring a long time ago." We see further evidence of this lack of caring in the episode "Product Recall," where he schemes to get a woman fired for a mistake he made, gathers money for her as a goodbye present, and then pockets the entire sum for his own profit.

Although Creed's ability to steal from others is well documented, it also appears he has a very strong interest in voyeurism and other deviant sexual behavior, as he demonstrates again and again throughout the series. He has a very casual attitude towards homosexuality, as he demonstrates in the episode "Gay Witch Hunt" where he reports that he made love to many women in the sixties "often outdoors, in the mud and rain" and "it's possible a man slipped in; there would be no way of knowing." His knowledge of various sexual positions is also shown in the episode "Diwali," where he perks up when Michael passes around photos from the Kama Sutra, and he lets everyone know that one particular position is known as "the union of the monkey." It is further suggested in the episode "The Promotion," that he and Meredith have been intimate, although when Meredith suggests this to him he appears oblivious. He also is known to make the women in the office uncomfortable with his excessive staring, as evidenced in the episode "The Coup," where he notices Pam has purchased some newer, more revealing clothing, and he goes to her desk and stares for quite some time, despite the fact that Pam is clearly uncomfortable.

His tendency towards voyeurism is also shown in an episode with former Stamford employee Hannah, who inadvertently exposes her breast to put milk in a baby bottle shortly after the two branches merged. Creed, sensing an opportunity, takes a snapshot of her breast and puts it on his computer. Later he is confronted about the picture, but takes this confrontation as admiration, and replies that he was "at the right place at the right time."

Perhaps Creed's creepiest sexual behavior occurs in the episode "Women's Appreciation", where we see Creed's fascination with hanging around the women's bathroom. When queried about this by the documentary crew, Creed reports that he is a "pretty normal guy who does one weird thing." He goes on to elaborate that "I go to the women's bathroom to do number two. I've been caught several times and I have paid dearly." Later in the episode, Phyllis describes how a man flashed her in the parking lot by exposing his genitals to her, to which an incredulous Creed replies that "the guy was just hanging brain, what's all the fuss?" He continues his plea later, insisting that "if that's flashing, then lock me up."

His criminal behavior is, in fact, so advanced that it is possible that he is not even Creed Bratton at all. This theory is supported by his revelation in a deleted scene from the episode "Product Recall," where he reports that he faked his own death a decade earlier "for tax reasons", and that all of his scheming has allowed him to draw benefits as his own widow. It seems to be a widely held belief in the office that he may not in fact be who he says he is, as evidenced in the episode "Did I Stutter" when Dwight shows Michael a flow chart of everyone in the office, and the name "Creed Bratton" is seen in quotation marks, suggesting they are also suspicious that he is not who he claims to be. The circumstances of this change in identity are perhaps clarified in the episode "Crime Aid," where Creed suggests to the camera that Creed Bratton was a man who mysteriously "disappeared" after stealing from him, whoever he actually is. The idea that he may have killed someone is also strongly implied in the episode "Murder," where Creed, who has shown up late to a murder mystery game Michael has set up, is told that there has been a murder and that he is the prime suspect. Creed responds in an extremely friendly manner, and then we see him sprinting to his car and peeling out of the parking lot, leading us to believe he feels his actual murder may have been uncovered.

Although Creed's drug use, stealing, and sexual deviancy have been well documented, it is also important to consider the fact that Creed may have some kind of delusional disorder, as his bizarre statements and behavior often suggest that he has had some kind of break from reality. One possible explanation may be that his prolonged drug use has damaged his brain, a theory made plausible by his own statement in a deleted scene from "Booze Cruise," where he reveals that as a result of his prolonged drug abuse he cannot concentrate for longer than 90 seconds. A possible diagnosis of drug induced psychosis is also supported by his proclamation to Toby in a deleted scene that he can put him in touch with a guy who can hook him up with "delicious coffee that you snort," and his ability to identify a number of different strains of marijuana when Dwight is interrogating him during the episode "Drug testing."

Regardless of whether or not it is actually drug-induced, Creed's strange behavior is certainly at a clinical level. One area of continuing speculation concerns Creed's ability to correctly identify his age. At one point we are told he is the same age as the real Creed Bratton, who was born in 1943, but Creed contradicts this on a couple of occasions throughout the series. In the episode "Fun Run" he talks about he will turn 82 on his next birthday, which could possibly be true given the fact that he previously revealed in the episode "The Injury" that he was in an iron lung as a teenager, indicating that his age may perhaps be quite advanced. Later Creed does a complete reversal about his age however, informing the crew that he will "be 30 in November." In support of this rather obvious lie, he dyes his hair with black ink from one of the printers, discusses his affection for Red Bull, and begins uses phrases such as "cool beans" and "later skater" around the office to convince everyone of his youth.

This is not the only incidence of Creed's confusion, as his story also changes about where he actually lives. In the episode "Product Recall" he tells us he was formerly a homeless man, and how he would do anything, including steal, to avoid being homeless again. At another point he tells the crew he lives in Toronto three days a week to take advantage of the welfare system, and sleeps under his desk the rest of this week. Directly contradicting this, he later tells Jim he lives "down by the quarry" and invites him to come and throw things down there with him.

Further evidence of Creed's possible dementia is demonstrated by his inability to remember names, something he demonstrates repeatedly throughout the series. Examples include referring to Stanley as "Sammy," Angela as "Andrea" and "the office bitch," Jim as "the tall guy, Andy as "Jim," Oscar as "Ace," Dwight as "Cheroot" and Meredith as "Mary Beth," "the red head" or "the chick Michael hit with the car." In the episode "The Convention" he forgets he knows Meredith at all, and reintroduces himself to her as if she had just started working there. The deficits of his short-term memory are also on full display in the episode "Casual Friday," where Jim and Creed spend the day playing board games together, and Creed offers to set his daughter up with Jim on a date. When Jim patiently explains to Creed that he is engaged to Pam, Creed then reveals he always thought Jim was gay, which leads to a very confused Jim asking why Creed would try to set him up with his daughter if he were gay. Jim's attempt to use logic with Creed appears to confuse him even more, and he finally remarks that he doesn't know why he would do something like that.

Creed's tendency to break from reality is not only demonstrated by his words however, as he also engages in bizarre behavior, as evidenced in the episode "Beach Games," where he catches a fish with his hands and then shows off the fish skeleton to the rest of the crew after eating it. His bizarre reaction to the world around him is also evident in the episode "The Carpet," where he smells the feces Todd Packer has deposited in Michael's office and asks pleasantly, "is someone making soup?"

Based on all of this evidence, it is therefore clear that Creed meets criteria for any number of diagnostic disorders. A therapist working with Creed would have to strongly consider his prolonged history of drug use, his anti-social behavior, his deviant sexuality, as well as his bizarre thoughts, words, and behavior. A therapist privy to *all* of

Creed's behavior would have to strongly consider whether Creed even belongs outside of an institution, as his prolonged history of exploiting others along with his bizarre behavior both call into question his fitness to continue to perform his activities of daily living. With this in mind, here is a psychological workup of the indomitable Creed Bratton.

Diagnostic Impressions-Creed Bratton

Axis I-292.82 Substance-Induced Persisting Dementia, 312.32 Kleptomania, 302.82 Voyeurism, 304.30 Cannabis Dependence

Axis I -301.7 Anti-Social Personality Disorder

Axis III-Missing Toe

Axis IV-Housing Problems, Lack of primary support group, spiritual problem (involvement in cults)

Axis V-Current GAF: 45 Last year 45

Michael Gary Scott

Michael Scott, the fearful leader of Dunder Mifflin Scranton and amateur improv comedian, has perhaps the most complicated psychological profile. He is the main character, and perhaps, the most imitated by people watching the show. We are drawn to his character because he has as many moments of genius as he does imbecility, all the while remaining mostly loveable. When talking about the makeup of his personality it is hard to know where to start, especially because Michael demonstrates something different in nearly every episode.

The self-proclaimed "World's Best Boss" Michael Gary Scott was born March 15, 1965 in Scranton, PA, which is believable seeing how he acts anything but traveled. But what about his parents? In an episode titled "Baby Shower," Michael mentions to Jan's test-tube baby, Astrid, that she will be fine without a father because he grew up without one. He never tells us anything more, perhaps because it is all that he knows. We never get to meet his mom, but during his short stint in the Michael Scott Paper Company we overhear one of their conversations. From the manner in which he speaks to his mother, it is quite clear she still parents him despite him being well into his forties. It is safe to assume, given the fact Michael seldom gets discouraged, even when he should be, that his mother may have had the patience of

Mother Theresa. We also learn later that he has a step-sister, with whom he is estranged, that is until recently. It is unclear exactly when she became part of the family, but we are made to believe Michael spent much of his childhood alone or at least left out.

Although Michael's childhood was seemingly sad, we get a glimpse of his talents as a child actor. In "Take Your Daughter to Work Day" Michael showcases his former talents in a video excerpt from an old children's program *Fundle Bundle*. During an interview on the show Michael speaks of his adult ambitions, mentioning he wants "100 Kids." One hundred children is an ambitious goal, even for a polygamist. It does not take a psychologist to see this as classic compensation: Michael feels like his family environment is empty and devoid of the childlike happiness, thus he looks to compensate by making a conscious decision to go as far in the other direction as he can. One hundred is a magical number for most children, as it sounds about as big as the universe.

It is evident that Michael probably had a lot of interests, and likely never saw too many of them through to fruition. As an adult he seems to be a Pittsburg Pirates fan, a Lebron James fan, and involved in many musical parodies. Michael goes so far as to create a full court basketball game in the warehouse during office hours. In the episode "Basketball" we see, that despite being an avid fan, he has little athletic talent or physical prowess. We also see that, while not in terrible physical condition, Michael even appears inept in running. In the Michael Scott's Dunder Mifflin Scranton Meredith Palmer Memorial Celebrity Rabies Awareness Pro-Am Fun Run Race for the Cure his arrogance or, perhaps his ignorance, puts him in the hospital as he over carbo-loads, refuses water, and becomes severely dehydrated. We see a very linear style of thinking, which is typical of early adolescent children. Some psychologists have estimated that a majority of adults fail to actually operate in the abstract cognitive realm as Piaget once suggested. Michael fits this profile, at least part of the time. He refused water during the race likening it to facing rabies. While it was a noble gesture, it certainly was not an intelligent one by anyone's standards.

Despite his lack of athletic talent, Jan makes it a point to compliment him on his ice skating and it is mentioned at least once in the episodes that he was a decent ice hockey player. However, in keeping with the Michael Scott way, he contradicts his own physical awkwardness and weakness by defeating Dwight in a fight at the dojo where he is an assistant to the Sensei.

No matter your take on Michael, we see inconsistencies that are difficult to explain, that is without the application of modern psychology. Being a precocious, active, and needy young boy, Michael likely required extra guidance when compared to his peers. We can see evidence of his mother's current involvement via a phone call to her while working for the Michael Scott Paper Company. Michael has trouble seeing things through, even as an adult. We seldom see Michael fully complete a plan or to have the foresight to see why some ideas ouglt not be pursued at all. This echoes of a child who has a limited attention span and trouble with his short-term memory. In the episode "Safety Training" Michael comes up with the idea to jump from the rooftop of the building to prove the severity of office place dangers like depression. He nearly jumps off the roof, had it not been for some quick thinking employees like Jim and Pam who ultimately coax him down with "presents". We also see in many episodes that he has to employ excessive mnemonic devices in order to remember people's names. He best demonstrates this skill, or lack thereof, in the episode "Lecture Circuit." By some means unknown to the viewers,

Michael's branch has performance numbers far surpassing the others. As requested by corporate, he travels to a handful of the poorly performing branches in hopes that some of his idiot magic could rub off on them. Michael, in an attempt to demonstrate how he remembers new people's names, focuses on stereotypical features with insensitive and misogynistic verbiage to remember otherwise unremarkable and ordinary people. While no one would approve of his methods, strangely they seem to work for him. This is a skill he likely learned early on in childhood, but failed to develop it into a more prosocial tool. Using these mnemonic devices could be crucial for a child with attention difficulties to thrive in school, at home, or other venues.

Often paired with impulsiveness or inattentiveness is clumsiness. Michael Scott is no stranger to avoidable injuries and faux pas. Perhaps no episode displays all of the characteristics associated with Adult Attention Deficit Hyper-Activity Disorder (ADHD) as well as "The Injury". In this episode we come to find out that Michael has, in fact, burned his foot on a George Foreman grill while attempting to wake himself with the smell of bacon. Just chew on that for a moment. If we tease this apart we have many things: forgetfulness, impulsive behavior, clumsiness, and overall physical and mental ineptitude. Each of these characteristics have a high correlation with ADHD, and Michael seems to encompass them all.

Although all of the previously mentioned characteristics seem to be the most apparent traits, with another look another it is his dependence upon others that becomes most obvious. Michael Scott yearns deeply for the approval of others, frequently to his own demise. He once referred to the office as something of a "fun place," despite his knowledge that corporate would be more concerned with productivity. We understand this emphasis on fun as a subtle ploy to win the hearts of his coworkers by manipulative means rather than choosing to lead by example. In nearly every episode there is a meeting, seminar, lecture, birthday party, or celebration of sorts. We get the impression he likely interrupts work time often, partially because of his bouts of ADHD and partially because of his incessant neediness.

Michael also dedicates copious amounts of his time trying to make his workplace his home. Other than the improv group he belongs to, which we later find out might use that term "belong" loosely, really has little going outside of the 9-5. We don't see or hear about any friends outside of the folks he works with. Perhaps this is why he constantly pesters couples like Jim and Pam with invitations to dinner dates. He desperately wishes to fit in and find his place, but just like at home in his earliest of years that place is too often occupied by him alone.

Based upon his psychological symptoms and inability to firmly connect with many people, he likely will invest in even the unhealthiest of relationships. Take for example his relationship with Jan. She at nearly every juncture sends him subtle and explicit cues that she does not have the same intentions in developing their relationship, yet Michael blindly carries on. She gives him but the fewest and smallest of nibbles to hang on to, which is just enough to keep him around. This behavior may admittedly say more about her own self-admitted psychopathology, but rest assured, Michael plays a role in it to. The overly dependent person attaches a majority of their self-worth and image to the few relationships he or she is a part of, thus influencing an over-investment of sorts. This sort of thing allows Michael to withstand much of the abuse Jan dishes out, as it is all for a good cause, and the thought of being alone is more than threatening to the delicate psyche he has. We might also say that his attraction to Jan has something to do with her power and ranking over him. His need to please could be best fulfilled by someone that is truly his cognitive superior.

Similarly, we see Michael attach to the temp Ryan. Michael looks to Ryan for style cues, maybe in hopes Ryan will look to him for guidance. Ryan may never agree, but it is evident Michael greatly wants Ryan to be his protégée. Having someone willing to admire him and learn from him could solidify Michael's sense of self. When Michael learns of Ryan's leapfrog promotion into corporate management, he attempts to explain this with an old eastern proverb where "the student overcomes the teacher." It is unfortunate that after his promotion Ryan pays no credence to Michael's tutelage. Even after Karma strikes Ryan and he is fired (Whoa!! Check it out You Tube Video), Michael scoops him up from a bowling alley and rehires him. Whether or not you'd consider his infatuation with Ryan romantic, the relationship constitutes dependency.

Despite all of the psychopathology he displays, Michael is equally endearing. No matter how much you start to hate him during an episode you badly want to see him succeed. Have you ever stopped and asked yourself why this may be so? Simply put, Michael is to the office as Lenny was to "Of Mice and Men." No matter how awkward, incapable, or insensitive he appears the motivating factor behind all that he does is good. Forgive him; he knows not what he does. Michael, for right or wrong, truly loves each and every employee in the office and there are few favors he would refuse a colleague. Whether it's negotiating Pam a job in sales during the buy-out of the Michael Scott Paper Company or forgiving those like Dwight who trespass against him, he is ultimately loveable.

If he is in fact so loveable, then why has he not been in a healthy and successful relationship? Truth be told with his level of pathology it would be difficult for someone to spend enough time with him to see the good and those who spend enough time with him might be quickly worn thin by his antics. Thus, Holly Flax. She was and is the perfect candidate for Michael. Her own slapstick style and inability to recognize social cues make them a perfect match. She works with Michael enough to get to know him, and not too long to where she is disgusted. With the help of Jim, the poor man's Don Juan, Michael learns to appropriately pursue his new love interest. Michael and Holly's story is a whirlwind romance cut short by Holly's sudden transfer to a different branch. We are made to feel quite sorry for

Michael after he loses Holly, but we always have hope she will come back, as it was a match made in Dunder.

After a series of short-lived relationships Michael continues to subconsciously compare each to Holly. None match that feeling. Eventually, Holly comes back into the picture and they rekindle an old flame. While it is not clear if they will ride off into the sunset forever, they will do so at least for tonight.

As Michael's time at the office comes to a close, we must look at indications for treatment of such a character. Mentioned several times, there are many pieces of his puzzle that contradict one another. He smoothly flows out of being an idiot to a genius and then subtly back. The first point of attack for any seasoned psychotherapist is a bit of good assessment. In his case we would want to do a plethora of test batteries, but none would be more important than an intelligence test. The question "what are we working with here?" could finally be answered. My guess is as good as any, but I don't see Michael Scott inside the middle of the bell curve, he will either prove to be a genius or putz.

We also do not know how anyone could adequately address all of his issues without totally deconstructing him as a person. No matter the case, we are at least given a glimpse into what therapy may need to look like for Michael. During the episode "Counseling" Michael is forced to undergo a therapy program with Toby in response to him violently spanking a fellow do-little employee, his nephew Luke in the previous episode "Nepotism." During the therapy sessions we see Michael as highly guarded and even nastier to Toby than usual. Finally, through back-channeled play therapy Toby gets Michael to start expressing his feelings. Michael refers to his step-father as his "mother's boyfriend…who she married," hinting to us that there are definitely some wounds there. He also reiterates something we've already concluded; he felt alone and quite sad as a child. Perhaps his early memory of his dog running away paints us the best picture. Toby asks him why he would not go to the park to look for him after he ran away and Michael responds "I thought he'd find a kid he'd like better," suggesting even his dog had trouble attaching to him. Michael has deepest psychological wounds in the office, which are evidenced by his behavior being the worst.

On a positive note, his relationship with Holly seems to be appropriate in a weird and quirky way. We learn that Michael needs someone to love him unconditionally and show him patience more than help provide him with insight or direction. Michael would do best with very expressive therapies that allow him to work in metaphors, softening the blow of the old injuries. Although positive social interaction should be encouraged, he might need adequate one-on-one time before he expands his newly formed skills.

Diagnostic Impressions-Michael Scott

Axis I- 314.01 Attention Deficit Hyperactivity Disorder, Combined Type, 3004 Dysthymic Disorder, Early Onset, with atypical features.

Axis II-301.9 Personality Disorder Not Otherwise Specified-Features of Dependent Personality Disorder, Borderline Personality Disorder, and Histrionic Personality Disorder. R/O 299.80 Pervasive Developmental Disorder Not Otherwise Specified.

Axis III-R/O Early childhood head trauma.

Axis IV-Severely limited appropriate social support

network as evidenced by over investment in work

associates lives, and upcoming career transition.

Axis V-GAF: 53 (Somehow he manages).

Pam Halpert

Although many of the characters that have been assessed for this project have had some serious psychological problems, it is important to note that not everyone on the show is so disturbed. Which brings us to the character of Pam, who is certainly one of the most likeable characters in the office, and a person who has changed a great deal over the course of the series. Much of Pam's story, particularly in the most recent seasons, is told in relation to her now husband Jim Halpert, who has been Pam's best friend and supporter since the beginning. Much of what ingratiates Pam to the viewers is her sense of vulnerability, and she is often a voice of sanity in an otherwise chaotic office environment.

When we are first introduced to Pam, she is a timid person, who is essentially resigned to living her life as a receptionist and living with her fiancé Roy, to whom she has been engaged for at least three years without actually setting a wedding date. We are given a glimpse of Pam's sensitivity almost immediately, when she begins crying in the very first episode "Pilot," when Michael pretends to fire her.

We get a glimpse of Jim Halpert's attraction to Pam in the second episode "Diversity Day," when, after a long day of putting up with

Michael's foolish activities, she falls asleep on Jim's shoulder, which he is clearly delighted with. Their feelings for each other continue to develop throughout the series, but this is an early indicator of Jim's thus far unrequited love for Pam.

But romance is still a long ways off for Jim and Pam, and made more complicated by Roy, who works in the warehouse and keeps Pam on a short leash. We see the first signs of tension between Jim and Roy in the episode "The Alliance," when Pam and Jim spend the day playing pranks on Dwight, and continue to grow closer as the day progresses. As they are laughing about this at the end of the day, Jim places his arms around Pam, which Roy sees and is seriously upset with, even going so far as to accuse Jim of "trying to cop a feel" on his fiancé. The tension between the two is also evident in the next episode "Basketball," where Jim and Roy get into a minor skirmish on the court as Jim attempts to impress Pam with his basketball prowess.

As the first season progresses, we continue to see that Jim and Pam have a very close friendship, although they are not close to taking it towards anything further. At this point in the series we continue to see a kind of sadness and vulnerability in Pam, and we as viewers begin to root for the idea that Pam and Jim will one day find a way to be together. Just when we think this might be possible, Jim begins to see Katie, a purse saleswoman from the Season 1 finale "Hot Girl," and we are left to wonder if things are ever going to work out for them.

The next time we see Jim and Pam together is in the first episode of the second season, "The Dundies," where we are given some indications that Pam feels as strongly about Jim as he clearly does for her. After a fight with Roy, Pam begins drinking heavily, and following an impassioned speech after receiving a Dundie for her tennis shoes, she kisses an ecstatic Jim directly on the lips. Although this alone could be chalked up to the alcohol, it briefly gets more serious when Pam attempts to communicate something important to Jim, although she is unable to finish the thought.

This sets an important tone for the character development of Pam, as we are given glimpses that she is a fairly unfulfilled and unhappy person, who vacillates between contemplating other alternatives for her life, and simply accepting her life for what it is. Her interactions with Jim give us a glimpse of what life could be like for Pam, as he continually encourages her in the directions of her dreams, although Roy is often quick to point out the negatives in these situations.

This dichotomy between Jim's encouragement and Roy's dream killing becomes especially clear in the episode "Boys and Girls," where Pam, when pressed by Jan, admits that she has dreamed of being an artist. Jan, hoping to identify new talent amongst the women of the branch, tells Pam about a graphic design program in New York that Pam would be eligible for. This episode marks an important turning point for Pam, as she describes a life where she is a working artist in a home where she is free to express herself creatively. She briefly allows herself to imagine becoming unstuck from the banality of her current existence, and to contemplate a glimpse of what life could be.

But immediately we see Pam's sadness return when Roy actively discourages such a move, which makes Jim angry enough to confront her, telling her "you're going to have to take a chance on something, sometime." Pam angrily tells him "she's fine with her choices," although we as viewers can see that she clearly is not In the final closing interview, Pam speaks to the camera, rationalizing that they don't even make her dream house in Scranton, which is a continuation of her explanation to Jim about being happy with her current existence.

Pam breaks down and cries as she says this however, which confirms for us that she has in fact been lying to herself about accepting her current life as it is. We as viewers can see that Jim would be an excellent alternative to Roy, as he is in many ways everything that Roy is not. In this regard it is important to think about this from a school of thought in psychology called "the stages of change", where a person may be in one of 6 stages as they attempt to change a particular behavior. Pam has now moved from the "pre-contemplation" phase, where a person cannot even see a problem, to the "contemplation" stage, where a person may know they need to change but are not yet ready to take action in this direction.

We are given evidence that Pam has at least contemplated what her alternative reality with Jim might look like in the episode "Sexual Harassment," where Pam's mom comes to town, and whispers to Pam, "which one is Jim?" which he overhears and is clearly pleased with. Jim and Pam reconnect in the episode "Office Olympics," where Pam talks about how creative Jim is when it doesn't pertain to work. The two are also flirtatious in the episode "The Fire," where Jim arranges a series of games designed for them to get to know each other a little better. Jim's girlfriend Katie shows up at the end of the episode, and Pam gives some clues that she clearly does not think Katie is the right girl for Jim, as she scoffs at some of Katie's answers to the questions that Jim has designed.

Jim and Pam have some additional conflict in the episode "The Fight," where he lifts her up in a playful manner, but takes this physical play a little too far, which upsets Pam who then yells at him. Jim is crushed by this perceived rejection, which again shows how far their unkacknowledged love has developed. They are at this point two people going through the motions of their lives while also deeply desiring to be together, and Jim resorts to the behavior of a little boy simply to get a chance to touch Pam and feel closer to her. Although she seems to feel the same way about him, she is also trying to maintain the impression that she is a loyal and honest girlfriend, which is part of why she rebukes Jim so strongly during the incident mentioned above.

Their affection for each other is also apparent in the episode "Christmas Party," where Jim puts together an elaborate Christmas gift for Pam which includes a number of mementos celebrating their time together. When given the choice, Pam chooses his gift over a very expensive Ipod, which again demonstrates their affection for each other. Psychologically, they both seem to be changing, gaining enough gratification from their relationship to find some happiness in their lives, despite the fact that destiny has not yet allowed them to be completely together.

The fates again intervene in the episode "Booze Cruise," when two important developments occur, which include Jim breaking up with Katie and Roy finally setting a date for he and Pam to be married. As is consistent with television formula, we see the characters who we most want to be together pulled further apart, and we are left to wonder if they are both doomed to lives of unrequited love and unfulfilled passion. One other important thing also occurs in this episode, as Jim confesses to Michael that he once had a crush on Pam.

Although Jim later bemoans this decision, on some level he has to know Michael will blab this information to everyone else, as is consistent with all of his previous behavior. Perhaps this is Jim's way of making the unconscious conscious, which Freud felt was one of the goals of therapy. Michael tells everyone about this in the episode "The Secret," which finally results in a conversation, however introductory, between Jim and Pam about the feelings that they have for each other. This is again clearly on display in the episode "Michael's Birthday," where they embark on a shopping trip, where we as viewers are given a glimpse of what their life together might be like.

"Casino Night," the final episode of the season, provides a pivotal moment for the character of Pam, as all of the pent up feelings between she and Jim finally bubble to the service. Jim, taking a chance he has been dreaming about for some time, professes his love for Pam, who tells him that she can't act on these feelings. Jim, undeterred by this rejection, gives her a kiss, which they both agree they've wanted to do for quite some time. Clarifying what this all means, they discuss this and Pam assures Jim that she still intends to marry Roy, which sends Jim reeling, and eventually both out of town as well as completely out of Pam's life for the time being.

At this point we perhaps begin to see Pam's life as something akin to the movie "Groundhog's Day." She knows that her current life is not working, but she needs to experience some new reality before she is actually ready to find happiness. In this regard Pam calls off her wedding to Roy, and begins to change from the meek and passive soul we have seen throughout the seasons, to a more confident and assertive person.

At this point we see Jim and Pam as living parallel narratives, he in Connecticut, and she back in Scranton. We see Jim in his new life, which he has created as a reaction to the heartbreak he experienced over Pam's rejection. He is beginning to pick up the pieces however, as he begins building a friendship with his co-worker Karen, which will eventually bloom into a romance. Meanwhile back in Scranton, Pam has begun to live as a single and independent woman. We finally see Jim and Pam reconnect again over the phone at the end of the episode "The Initiation," and the rapport between them is quickly reestablished.

Jim and Pam finally reconnect in person when the branches merge together, although things are awkward between them at first, as Jim struggles to balance his relationship with Karen and his friendship with

Pam, which will be a theme throughout this season. Pam, who has high expectations about Jim's return, is clearly saddened by this development, and the whole season we see Pam in a similar situation to Jim in the first two seasons, where she must suffer as she watches the person she loves in a relationship with someone else.

Much like Pam in the early season, however, we soon see that Jim is not with the one he loves, a feeling he intimates to Michael in "Benihanna Christmas." We eventually see how much anguish Pam is in over this whole situation in the next episode, where she begins sobbing at the thought of being estranged from Jim. A highly discouraged Pam, now experiencing intense feeling of loneliness, eventually regresses to old ways at Phyllis' wedding, and begins dating Roy again, which also upsets Jim. Pam's decision to get back with Roy quickly backfires on her in the episode "Cocktails," where Pam, trying to access a more honest side of herself, informs Roy that she kissed Jim which results in him trashing a bar as well as their final breakup.

Pam's transformation into a more honest person is finally realized in the episode "Beach Games," where she makes an impassioned speech in front of the entire group about how much she misses Jim and would like to reconnect with him. This escalates a growing sense of tension between Pam and Karen, and Jim must make a critical decision about what he wants when he is offered a chance to move to New York. While interviewing for this job, Jim sees a thoughtful note Pam has written for him, and realizes that the life he wants is with Pam back in Scranton. In the final scenes of season three, we see Jim finally ask Pam on a date, just as she is explaining to the camera that they weren't destined to be together. She happily accepts, and we see Pam may get the thing she has been wanting the most for so many years.

In the later seasons, we get to see how Pam has indeed been redeemed by love. Being with Jim has given her a new kind of confidence, and we slowly see a transformation in her from a sad and lonely person to someone who is happy, poised, and self-assured. At the end of Season Five, we see that Pam's life is about to change even further, as it is revealed to the audience that she and Jim are going to have a baby. They eventually get married in a hilarious and touching ceremony, and we see Jim and Pam as a happy and collaborative couple as the seasons progress.

Still, questions remain about Pam from a psychological perspective. Why was she so quick to give up on her art school dreams? How will her failure in this regard affect her sense of self-efficacy moving forward? Is being a mother and a wife in an unfulfilling career suffice, or will she grow bored and restless of this one day? Is finding and being with her soul mate enough for Pam? Ultimately we may never find out any of these things, but in the confines of the series, we see that Pam has found her redemption though her love with Jim. Perhaps being a mother will also be a source of great happiness for Pam, as she and Jim have thus far derived a great deal of joy in watching their daughter CeCe grow up. Whatever happens, we have seen Pam emerge into a completely changed person, as she has accessed a completely new side of herself through her interactions with Jim.

Diagnostic Impressions-Pam Halpert

Axis I- 296.26 Major Depressive Disorder, Single Episode In Full Remission.

Axis II V71.09 No Diagnosis

Axis III- None noted

Axis IV- Occupational problem, Problems with primary support group (parent's divorce, mother's relationship with her boss.)

Axis V- GAF 75

Andrew Baines Bernard

Although Andrew Baines Bernard is the first-born son of privilege, he is probably known best for his sharp, yet quirky attire. In nearly every episode we see him mixing plaids with suedes and bright colors with corduroy in a "metro sexual meets frat boy look." Andrew is a self proclaimed ladies man extraordinaire, but we get to witness a much different picture throughout his character's development.

Perhaps it is best to start at the beginning and learn the story of the real Andrew Bernard. We learn, in a scene that failed to make the cut, in "Chair Model," that Andy was born Walter Bernard, Jr. after his father. Shortly after the birth of his younger brother, his parents felt Andrew's junior better embodied the strong core masculine values they'd like to associate with the patriarchal family namesake, and thus gave the name to his younger brother. Using a baby book, his mother and father selected "Andrew." As is often the case with oldest children, Andrew faced a dethronement by his younger sibling. That is to say, older children are often threatened psychologically by younger children. Parents often shift the focus, or at least split it, which frequently wrecks the delicate psychological structure of children not best prepared for the sibling addition. We know that Andy is not overly masculine or "tough" by most standards and we know his parents often pampered him, thus he was not independent enough to face the dethronement. As is common in most well-to-do families, the oldest patriarch is to settle into some great wealth and inherent the fortunes of fathers' past. Being overlooked as Andrew was can be reckoned to Alfredo in *Godfather.* He is destined for a life devoid of the initial privileges one expected. This is the beginning and perhaps the most profound influence in "Nard Dog's" psyche.

Despite being passed over, Andrew still has a "silver spoon life" by most standards. Although we know less about his childhood, we do know much about his adult life. He first appears in "The Gay Witch Hunt" and his excessive bragging is an evident mainstay in his character. "I went to Cornell, you ever heard of it?" is the single most memorable quote from Mr. Bernard. We also see in his first episode his boundless attempts to fit in with the top social group. In the same episode he aptly calls Jim Halpert "Big Tuna" because he ate a tuna sandwich on his first day. Andy uses nicknames to forgo the long process of establishing respect and admiration – likely influenced by his early temperament and lack of patience thereafter. Everyone is probably guilty of trying to achieve quick intimacy, but none have the plethora of tactics to do so like Andy. Little does he know that Jim sees

him as a replacement for his old foe, Dwight.

Despite seeing a minor lack of patience and the remnants of a

pampered child, we aren't exposed to his temper until Jim plays his

first prank. Likely worn tired by constantly being referred to as "Big

Tuna," Jim places Andy's calculator in a jello mold.   When Andy

opens his drawer to run a few numbers he finds his ten key secured in

plate full of green jello. Within seconds he stands up and begins to

threaten his coworkers. This is the first of many overreactions to

environmental stimuli. Most would appreciate the humor in Jim's

jokes, but for Andy such things are taken as a threat to his identity,

most assuredly opening up his earliest wound, the one where his name

was taken away from him. For Andy, feeling powerless is much less

tolerable than it might be for other folks around the office.

Perhaps Andy makes himself an easy target for bullying and pranks

by excessively bragging, making others subject to his impromptu a

cappella renditions of pop songs, or simply by overdressing for a

business casual work place. Nevertheless, he seems to miss obvious

social cues that the average Joe would be aware of. In the episode "The

Return," Jim, minus his antithesis Dwight, again is pestered by Andy's desperate and perpetual ploys at winning the affection of his peers. During the episode he unceasingly annoys the office with a home recording of his a cappella group that he formatted into a ring tone. Jim, with the help of others, hides Andy's phone in the ceiling. This throws fuel on the fire, one that's already burning for years inside of poor Nard Dog. Near the end of the episode his pot boils over and he punches a hole in the wall. The rest of the office sits stunned as the episode concludes. It is unclear if they fear for their own safety or are just in awe at watching a grown man regress to an angry child.

Despite his temper, Andy has many redeemable qualities. With a childlike innocence, an uncanny ability to harmonize, and his usually prim and proper style, many are won over by Andrew Bernard. Unfortunately, we see a general lack of talent for what most consider a menial job. In the episode "Koi Pond," the two lowest grossing salespersons are forced to hit the road for "cold calling" in efforts to win new clients and increase their numbers. We see that most of Andy's sales attempts, with little help from Pam, fail to win over potential clients. Although, both of their sales are low, Pam seems more concerned than Andy. We are left to wonder what role his parents have in his lack of motivation. In the episode "Secretaries' Day," we learn that his parents still pay his credit card bills. Which makes sense, Brooks Brothers is out of the budget of a Dunder Mifflin man. Earlier, in a deleted scene from "Branch Wars," we learn that Andy's parents donated a building to Cornell. This helps us understand how someone who was proclaimed to be "drunk the whole time" and spend all his free time in an a cappella group, "Here comes treble," could actually graduate on time from an Ivy League institution such as Cornell.

To get a deeper appreciation of Andy's psyche we need to understand more of his peer relationships. In his first episode, "The Gay Witch Hunt," Andy introduces Karen by suggesting he has had intimate relations with her, but she is a bit of a loose cannon. This is classic projection, which is best described as a person believing they are looking out of a window when in truth they are gazing into a mirror. Andy's rant about Karen foreshadows more about his own behavior than that of his colleague. In addition to trying to look cool in Jim's eyes, it is a childlike approach to office politics. Throughout the show's short production at the Stamford branch, we don't see Karen act disgusted or threatened by Andy, which may tell us he has at least a minimal set of skills to make friends.

After Stamford is absorbed by Scranton, Andy's character becomes more noteworthy. We later observe him desperately attempt to court Angela, the very rigid and cold accountant. In discussions with other office members he makes his attraction to qute clear. In "Launch Party" Andy entices Dwight with some locker room banter. Unbeknownst to Andy, likely because he just came from Stamford or because of he always seems oblivious to social cues, he engages in a somewhat sexual chat with the former lover of Angela. Dwight, still working to protect their somewhat secretive past, plays patsy as Andy approaches some off-color commentary about his lust for Angela. While this is not completely uncommon for men to chat about, most reserve this sort of thing for the times outside of work and with good friends.

In the episode "Product Recall," Jim and Andy are asked to go to a local school and pacify complaints about a racy watermark that was left on several reams of paper. Shortly upon entering the school, Andy sees the girl he is dating. Confused, as he believed her to be much older, he attempts to approach her and make a huge fuss. Persuaded by Jim to calm down, he makes passive-aggressive comments about her to a school official. Jim ends up smoothing over Andy's mess by pledging to buy ad space in the school yearbook. Andy revealed that he met her at a local eatery he frequents, and never believed her to be a minor. Regardless of knowing or not knowing her exact age, she holds the type of employment usually reserved for part-time high school and college kids, all of which are too young to be appropriate mates for him. We do glean some important psychological information here, no Andy is not a sexual predator, he does not fit that profile, rather his innocence and naiveté clue us into him being at a younger psychological age than chronological one. This we might attribute to a critical development period being stunted by over-protective or pampering parents.

Although he later attempts a more pro-social relationship with the new office secretary Erin, he goes about it again in a childlike way. Over the course of a few episodes he befriends Pam and begs her to aid him in starting a relationship with him. He speaks much kindlier about Erin, and truly seems to adore her beauty and quirky style, but ultimately their relationship is ended by Erin's inability to accept Angela as his former lover and fiancé. At this point, Andy seems to be devastated, and to add to his downward spiraling depression he finds her to be dating the new Sabre manager Gabe.

The loss of this relationship was very difficult for Andy. At multiple points he attempts to win her over again, despite her relationship with Gabe. No better example can be found than in the episode "Andy's Playbill." He is the headlining star of the musical play *Sweeny Todd*, and tries to get Erin to the performance so he may win her over with song. While we are endeared by Andy's big sweet heart, we also see he is slowly losing touch with reality.

Slowly, but surely, Andy starts to grow up in front of our eyes. As he is exposed to many things that he was once sheltered from he learns to be more independent. We start to appreciate Andy, although, we cannot help but be annoyed by him sometimes. Whatever the verdict is on Andy, he becomes less of a nuisance and more of a friend to many in the office. This is best evidenced by his friendship with Darryl. In the beginning of their friendship Andy reverts back to his old ways of annoying people, but with the encouragement of a good friend he learns to tone it down.

This is not the first time Andy has tried to turn over a new leaf. In the episode "Safety Training," marking his return from anger management, he asks the office to refer to him as "Drew" hinting at starting a new anger-free identity. While it is not completely successful, we do not see any more large scale blow-ups from him as we once did. He appears much calmer and more collected throughout many of the subsequent episodes. We really are made to believe that "Nard Dog" and his million other nicknames, is quite unsure of his true identity. In the episode "Gossip," Michael starts several rumors to muddy the water for the real info he leaked about Stanley. At some point Michael tells other office employees that one of their coworkers is in fact gay. We witness Andy's lack of comfort with this accusation, as he is not completely sure about his sexuality and sexual orientation. Finally, at the end of the episode he learns that they are all rumors, and calms himself down.

To understand Andy's response to treatment, we needn't look farther than his stint in anger management. His five week course and therapy seems to have adequately addressed the triggers leading to his explosions. I believe his earliest childhood wound of having his name and status stripped from him must have at least been addressed inadvertently. One must also be careful to help Andy make a lifelong recovery from his anger; something that is expressed outwardly during his outbursts and inwardly with his low feelings of self-worth that are often compensated for by bragging. We learn that Andy is not completely cured in "Sex Ed." While teaching a seminar to his colleagues on sex, he is demoralized by his peers reactions and throws a pizza at the wall. Luckily for Nard Dog he has the support of Darryl to sooth him before it turns into an all out explosion. This tells us that Andy also feels best when he is supported by a few people close to him.

We are led to believe that Andy has the resources and verbal skills to best utilize insight based talking therapies. He also is very creative, loving, and has several hobbies. We see his love of music spur him to solidify a friendship with Darryl, who is otherwise an inaccessible friend. His friendships should be encouraged and role play might be beneficial, to ensure he does not revert back to being annoying to get attention from others.

Despite all of his hobbies and strengths, he must continue to address his earliest of wounds in therapy. Likewise, good therapy should include reparenting Andy in order to improve his health self-confidence, and maturity.

Diagnostic Impressions-Andrew Bernard

Axis I- 312.34 Intermittent Explosive Disorder, 313.82 Identity
Problem, 309.0 Adjustment Disorder with Depressed
Mood.

Axis II- V71.09 No Diagnosis

Axis III- None per client's report

Axis IV- Recent termination of romantic partnership

Axis V- Current GAF: 68

Dwight Kurt Schrute, III

Although he is not the number one man or the go-to-guy, Dwight K. Schrute sits at Michael's right hand, and sometimes at his foot when Michael has one of his mishaps with the bedside George Foreman. He is the one man in the office with a style truly based on efficiency and not aesthetics. Donned in a short-sleeved dress shirt, devoid of facial hair, with a yellow tie and large glasses, Dwight astonishes us with his many quotes during the documentary interviews. Other than a short stint at Staples, Dwight has been a loyal servant to Dunder Mifflin. In fact, in the episode "Traveling Salesman" he admits one of his life goals was to die at Dunder Mifflin in his chair. Despite his loyalty and drive to reach the top, we are left to wonder about many specifics from his childhood.

Although we never see Dwight's parents in any of the episodes, we do see his cousin Mose and hear references of a grandfather still surviving in another country. It is almost certain that Dwight comes from a strict German household, and by strict I mean something that was influenced by the 3rd Reich. Dwight never comes out and declares his allegiance to anything other than the office, but he makes reference to his grandfather being in an Allied Prison Camp during WWII and currently surviving in Argentina somewhere. We take this to mean that his family had ties to the Nazi party and after the war his grandfather likely fled prosecution by finding refuge in South America like many SS officers of that time did. Details about Dwight's history always seem to be mentioned in passing and seldom are the focus of major episode themes. In "Take Your Daughter to Work Day," Michael in passing tells the children that Dwight's grandmother was a Nazi war criminal. This information easily passes most viewers radar as we are drawn to more important details of the episode.

Although Dwight says very little about his German heritage, he is more transparent about his Amish influences. In the episode "Office Olympics," we learn of cousin Mose's backwards living, and are given a first-hand view of the two drastically different life styles Dwight lives. We never hear that Mose is Amish, but there is reference to some maternal ancestors living the Amish life style.

On the one hand Dwight Kurt Schrute III is a ruthless, yet polite, businessman (Beet Farmer), and on the other he is just a ruthless swindler, who would sell ice to Eskimos (Paper Salesman). No matter the time of day he is the eternal businessman at heart, and sometimes we see both his businesses overlap, like in the episode "Money" when Jim and Pam stay at the Beet Farm's Bed and Breakfast.

In addition to Dwight's possible ethnicities he tells us of his birth order. Dwight was the dominant one in a pair; he actually absorbed his twin before birth, claiming to have "the strength of a grown man and a baby." We see Dwight take on the values of an oldest child in his care taking of Michael, but his drive to overcome and surpass his coworkers seems more like that of a youngest child. Nonetheless, Dwight seems to have better developed his kinesthetic skills and book smarts and left the social and emotional intelligence in the trunk of his firebird along with some throwing stars, survival knife, and goose meat.

In some of Dwight's blogs we learn the harsh conditions in which the Schrute men were reared. Dwight spoke fondly of getting to swim for a few hours before his 14 hr shifts in the beet field. As we learn more about the development of narcissism, we understand the mirroring and validation that is necessary for a strong sense of self form. It is safe to assume that Dwight formed too strong of a sense of self. His narcissism was less likely to have formed from over-admiration by his family, and more likely from a lack there of. We mustn't underestimate the need for children to get consistent, encouraging, and fair feedback. We must assume that little of this was given from a stern father with high expectations of his children. Likely Dwight's unrelenting work ethic comes from a passion to please his father and is then transferred to individuals above him in the work place. The childlike elements in Dwight's personality also manifest themselves as Dwight constantly seeks feedback from his one superior in the office, Michael. Although Dwight's narcissism makes him believe he holds skills and abilities superior to the boss, his wounded child cannot help but seek approval.

Similarly, Dwight has a thirst for power that can never be fully quenched. There is no secret that the meager title of "Assistant to the Regional Manager" is neither astute nor royal enough for him. To boost his sense of ego, and not to be a responsible citizen, Dwight volunteers some of his spare time with the local police department. Although it is quite clear that he plays a minuscule role in the police department, it does not stop him from being the office braggart. In fact, Dwight is so convinced of his greatness, and natural power over others, in the "Conflict Resolution" episode it is revealed the he plays a game called "Second Life," where he is essentially the same character on the show and game. His avatar looks identical to him, pursues the same work and hobbies, and only holds the additional ability to fly. Dwight's fantasies of flying must be seen as conscious wish to power over others.

One of Dwight's most loveable qualities would have to be his loyalty to Michael and the company; however, his own narcissistic need for power is enough for him to engage in political games, even against coworkers with whom you think he is in love with. In the "Traveling Salesman" episode, taking a cue from Angela – his affectionate "monkey" – he tries to throw Michael under the bus to the corporate boss, Jan. Dwight will not break his loyalty to Angela, even to reconcile things with his mentor and self-acclaimed best friend, Michael Scott. This power play ended up getting Dwight temporarily fired and later earned him the chore of Michael's laundry.

Dwight's infinite self-resourcefulness, wild sales tactics, and hatred for Jim are readily available for observation by the common viewer. One must risk delving in below the surface to have a deeper appreciation for his psychological character. Many of his social relationships in the office are hierarchical, socially inappropriate, childish, or overly-competitive. We never really get to know the true nature of Dwight's intelligence. In the "Survivorman" episode, Dwight cautiously watches Michael from a distance, and eventually applies his affinity for survival and knowledge of edible shrubbery to intervene in Michael's filming before he eats poisonous plants. Yet in other episodes like "The Delivery" Dwight seems to be more of jack of all trades and master of none when he destroys Jim and Pam's kitchen during a rehab project. His genius is only masked by his madness, rendering viewers' appetites for concrete answers very unsatisfied.

To accurately assess Dwight and his true mental condition, we must first decipher the many odd relationships he has with people inside and outside of the office. In the office Dwight usually splits his time running errands for Michael, sneaking around with Angela, or engaging in pranks with Jim and Pam. Outside of the office Dwight is primarily a loaner, choosing to spend most of his free time managing his agrotourism business or perhaps playing table tennis. One great example of Dwight interacting with other adults outside of work is in the "Initiation" episode when cousin Mose assists him with some of the hazing to be done to Ryan during sales training. The dynamics between Mose and Dwight are unhealthy at best. Dwight controls Mose like an indentured servant and outcast, despite him possibly being Dwight's closest surviving family member. In analyzing his relationship patterns, it seems that Dwight only treats those who have an ability to increase his status with respect and cooperation. If you don't hold the key to Dwight earning a promotion, then it is best to get out of his way. We also see how quickly he turns on Michael after he is falsely given power in "The Traveling Salesman."

It is no surprise to learn that Dwight also is a misogynist, judging women only for their breading qualities and lack of physical prowess. "Reject a woman, and she will never let it go. One of the many defects of their kind. Also, weak arms," as evidenced in the episode *The Coup.* In unison with previous arguments, treating women as objects, especially breeding objects, is a tale-tale sign of narcissism. Many narcissists only see their women as objects they own and not people they cooperate with.

Jim is seen as Dwight's biggest enemy, and perhaps rightfully so, as Jim earns a promotion over Dwight just before the company is bought out by Sabre despite Dwight's astounding sales records. In all, we must understand the battles between Jim and Dwight if we are to truly understand the Schrute psyche. From the earliest of episodes Jim, with the help of Pam, plays multiple tricks and pranks on Dwight. Whether it was pretending Dwight was getting correspondences from the CIA, his future self, or a super computer, it did nothing else but fuel the paranoid fire burning brightly in the depths of Dwight's mind. Perhaps some of the fears Dwight has, that people are out to get him, are more than just remnants from his imagination. It could also be a familial value to treat others in such an unfriendly manner. It is almost as if

Dwight learned from his family that people have something to take away from you or they know dark secrets that will assuredly be used to bring down your success. We certainly have a case of this with the family's ties to the Nazi party and war crimes. Being influenced by a family on the run can toil and skew the psyche of children.

More evidence of diagnostic considerations outside of narcissistic personality disorder is evident, namely deeply psychotic axis one symptoms. We have made the case for Dwight's rampant paranoia: paranoia for the world coming to an end and a need to rely on his survival techniques or all individuals must be seen as enemies or superiors. This mindset defaults individuals to perceive an otherwise neutral environment as hostile and the demands of ordinary life as "too much." But what other symptoms do we see? We see evidence of this in his off-putting knowledge of animal mating rituals. He lets us know in the "Product Recall" episode that the animals in the caricatures seem to enjoy the sex because of "their smiles." Attributing human characteristics to non human animals can be a marker for how far one has truly lost touch with the shared common sense and reality.

Dwight also has other habits that could be of concern to a mental health clinician. Namely, during many of his interviews he appears to be asking himself most of the questions and readily responding. We notice with his eye movements that he is not communicating with the interviewer as much as himself. There is perhaps no better example of this loss of touch with reality than the first episode of season four "Fun Run" when Dwight answers the unasked questions about Jim. While he starts out making us think he is truly sad for Jim's departure, he quickly shifts to feeling hatred for his old foe. While it is unclear if this talking to himself comes with auditory hallucinations, it certainly warrants a deeper look shall we ever get the opportunity to work with him in vivo.

After all the psychological assessments are complete we are still left to answer the question of nature v. nurture. What caused Dwight to be the oddest tool in the shed? We are given one clue, in the episode "The Injury." Soon after the office learns of Michael's latest blunder, burning his foot on a George Foreman grill while trying to cook bacon from bed, Dwight being the good servant he is, or perhaps it is his thirst for feedback and praise, hastily races out of the Dunder Mifflin parking lot, only to slam his Firebird into a large telephone pole.

During this episode we observe major changes in Dwight's character and personality structure, all likely attributed to his concussion. He went so far as to befriend enemies, play nice with others, and generally have a pleasing and trusting disposition. If not for fear of death, I am sure some of the his office coworkers may have chosen to leave him in his injured state. We can thus deduce that Dwight, being a precocious young boy, working around much machinery conducive to injuries, and being involved in wrestling and later in martial arts, may have actually suffered multiple unreported head traumas. Unfortunately we never get to validate this theory with momma or papa Schrute.

In discussing Dwight's prognosis or likely response to treatment, we have a few mitigating factors: 1. His deeply ingrained personality structure which will not mend well with most traditional therapies, and 2. His previous positive encounters with some of the simplest psychological interventions. Jim is able to train Dwight using old behavioral principles of association. In "Phyllis's Wedding" Jim spends several days making a bell sound with his keyboard and immediately giving Dwight an Altoid, until he has no more. This may be a good indicator for behavioral interventions, besides Dwight will do almost anything for the possibility of a reward. There is also more data to support a case that he will be amendable via "hypnosis." In "The Initiation" episode, Dwight requests an extra few minutes in Jim's car so he can listen to "Kick Start My Heart." What might be happening is that Dwight may able to find comfort in the near trance-like state many people experience while listening to music. Although it is hard to say just how things would ultimately transpire in therapy, he would make a case study for the ages.

Diagnostic Impressions-Dwight Schrute

Axis I-295.30 Schizophrenia, Unspecified Pattern, Paranoid Type, R/O 299.80 Aspergers Disorder

Axis II- 301.81 Narcissistic Personality Disorder

Axis III- Complex Concussion as diagnosed by General

Axis IV-Recent loss of romantic relationship, Work-related stress, loss of economic resources

Axis V-Current GAF: 53

Meredith Palmer

As an Irishman, I've always had a little soft spot for Meredith, despite, or perhaps because, she is a raging alcoholic, a nymphomaniac, and often says things totally inappropriate for an office setting. I feel like I've seen (been) Meredith a time or two in my life, and we all can probably relate to the archetype of the hard-drinking colleague who comes in begging for people to keep the noise down after a night of over service. Meredith takes it to an art form though, and her antics both in and outside of the office are certainly worth some further examination.

Although it is hard to imagine the show without Meredith talking about drinking, her problems with alcohol were given no mention at all during the first season of the show. We are however given some information about her health problems, including the fact that she has had a hysterectomy. This is extremely confusing for Dwight, who believes this procedure indicates she has no vagina. Those that have seen the entire series know that this is of course false, as Meredith continues to get a great deal of use from her vagina throughout the series.

We also find out as the series progresses that Meredith is a parent, although we soon see that this situation is far from ideal. In episodes such as "Take Your Daughter to Work Day" we find that she has custody of her son, Jake, who we quickly find out is a juvenile delinquent who has had a number of problems at school. We also find out that she has a daughter named Wendy, but that she lives with Meredith's ex-husband who has custody of her. We also find out he left her for a garbagewoman, and how her kids now refer to this woman as "mom."

It is season two where we as viewers are first told of Meredith's drinking problem, including the fact that she has joined Alcoholics Anonymous. We also see her begin the bargaining practice regarding her pledge to quit drinking. In this season she references various New Year's resolutions she has made to quit drinking, but also how she has failed each time she has pledged this. We later see her adjust her goal of total abstinence, and she eventually makes a half-hearted pledge to stop drinking alcohol "during the week." This season differs from others, as it suggests Meredith has at one point in her life tried to quit drinking, which is not referenced and does not seem to be her goal at all as later seasons develop.

It is also in season two where we are first introduced to Meredith's promiscuity, which is highlighted in the episode "Booze Cruise," where she has sex with Captain Jack, who she has just met a short while before. It is also in this episode where we see Meredith has little fear of exposing herself in public, as she is seen dancing topless (except for a life preserver) following her sexual dalliance with the captain. A deleted scene from the episode "Email Surveillance" has her showing her breasts, which she does again after getting drunk at the Christmas party and flashing Michael, who has the presence of mind to take a picture of. Her promiscuity is again highlighted in a deleted scene from the season finale "Casino Night" where she tells the documentary crew that she does not remember most of the men she has had sex with while she is drinking.

Much of Meredith's sexual energy is directed to the pursuit of Jim Halpert, who usually appears visibly uncomfortable when Meredith makes sexually suggestive remarks with him in mind. In the episode "The Job," Jim comes in with a completely new look which includes a totally new hairstyle, which a lustful Meredith immediately refers to as "crazy hot." Although this was enough to make Jim apprehensive, she continues the harassment by telling him to "turn around" so that she can "see him from all angles." She continues her pursuit in the episode "Fun Run," where she is hit by Michael in his car, which leads to her being placed in a cast which extends around her genitals and entire pelvic area. She later asks Jim to sign her pelvis, and with a sexy whisper says, "I'll read this when I get home," implying she will be sexually fantasizing about Jim when they part company.

Although Meredith's sexual harassment of Jim continues throughout the series, there is at least one incident where her sexual behavior crosses from simple promiscuity to borderline prostitution. In a discussion of business ethics that was spurred by Ryan's behavior in the previous season, Meredith candidly admits that she has been having sex with Bruce Meyers, another company's supplier so the office could get a discount on various products. Meredith doesn't stop there however, and further offers that the exchange of sex for services also includes gift certificates for Outback Steakhouse. When queried about this, a defiant Meredith asks Holly, "Have you ever has sirloin steak honey?" making it clear that she is not at all ashamed of her behavior. When a visibly shaken Michael tries to help her out of the situation by giving her an alternative scenario to the sex for services trade-off story, she defies him as well, stating, "No, I wouldn't have done it if it wasn't for the discount paper, there's not a lot of fruit in those looms."

Considering that Meredith references the goal of quitting drinking early on in the series, we see that towards the later seasons she has totally abandoned this goal, as both her drinking and sense of denial about this drinking continue to increase. This is highlighted in the episode "Moroccan Christmas," where Meredith (with considerable help from Michael) begins to imbibes massive amounts of alcohol, which leads to her belly dancing while under the influence, and eventually setting her hair on fire.

Following this incident, Michael attempts a Mormon intervention, but Meredith is again defiant, and states flatly that she refuses to quit drinking. An exasperated Michael then pretends he is taking her to a bar, when he in fact intends to "make a deposit" by dropping her off at an alcohol rehabilitation center. In one of the series funniest moments, Michael drags a terrified Meredith, quite literally kicking and screaming, to the front door of the center, only to be informed he can't check someone in against her will.

In the seventh season, we find that Meredith's behavior has had some negative consequences, as she reveals in the episode "Sex Ed" that she has genital herpes. For those that are familiar with Meredith's pattern of behavior, this comes as no surprise, as her judgment and decision making has continued to get progressively worse as the show continues. In formulating Meredith's diagnostic workup, it is therefore important to note this.

Diagnostic Impressions-Meredith Palmer

Axis I- 303.90, Alcohol dependence, 302.90 Sexual Disorder NOS, V61.20 Parent-Child Relational Problem

Axis II- Borderline features noted

Axis III- Hysterectomy, Genital Herpes, Broken Pelvis, Rabies.

Axis IV- Problems with primary support group

Axis V Current GAF 55 Last Year 60

Jan Levenson

Perhaps no character on the show has seen their mental health decompensate more over the course of the show than Jan, whose fall from grace was alternatively hilarious and cringe-worthy over the course of several seasons. Most of Jam's decline coincided with her increasing involvement with Michael, and piecing out what part of her behavior was exacerbated by this relationship is important in coming up with her potential diagnosis.

When we first meet Jan, she is presented as a very well put together corporate executive from New York, whose style and poise indicate that she commands a great deal of respect. How much respect she actually commands however, is almost immediately called into question in the first episode, where Michael's incorrigible friend Todd Packer insults her over the phone, and, unbeknownst to him she hears every word of this. The tone of Jan's disapproval with Michael's work performance is set early in the series, and is a theme that runs through the first few seasons.

A significant change in their relationship occurs in the Season Two episode "The Client," where she and Michael are tasked with taking a potential client played by Tim Meadows out to dinner. Jan makes it clear to Michael that he is to let her take the lead throughout the evening, which leads to him quietly saying "power trip" under his breath, which aggravates her even more. Against Jan's wishes, Michael selects his beloved Chili's for the meeting place, and while there begins acting foolishly, including telling a series of uncomfortable jokes and singing the "Baby Back Ribs" theme from a Chili's commercial.

But nothing in this evening unfolds as we expect. We find out almost immediately that Jan is now divorced, which leads to a series of awkward inquiries from Michael that inexplicably seems to further ingratiate him to the client, who, against very long odds, enjoys Michael's sense of humor and general perspective on life. Jan grows tired of the rapport between the two, and begins drinking alcohol, which is a decision that will later come back to haunt her.

The whole situation ends with Michael securing the deal with the client, which leads to an ecstatic Jan, who has now had several drinks, passionately kissing Michael in the parking lot. We later find out that they retired back to Jan's hotel, where, according to Michael's revelation to the documentary crew, they "made out." Michael immediately begins sending mixed signals about the whole situation, admonishing Dwight to show her respect as a boss, while immediately referring to her as both "soft and sexy."This sets up a pattern where Michael continually reveals things about he and Jan that both mortifies and irritates her.

The next morning Jan, now filled with intense regret about the entire incident, asks Michael if he intentionally got her drunk, and even suggests the possibility that he may have slipped something in her drink. Meanwhile the rumors about she and Michael's rendezvous has already begun to spread around the office, which is truly Jan's worst fear realized in terms of maintaining the respect necessary to effectively do her job.

Jan's mistake with Michael continues to haunt her for several episodes, including in the following episode "Performance Review," where a theme is established where Michael now considers Jan his girlfriend, whereas she clearly regrets the incident and wants nothing further to do with Michael romantically. For those who have seen the entire series, we know that this is of course not totally true, and we see that Jan's internal struggle, which will eventually almost completely transform her into a state of ruin, has now begun.

In examining Jan's anger at the situation, we see that she repeatedly scolds and admonishes Michael for continuing to pursue the situation, and she rejects him over and over as he continues to drop innuendos and advances in her direction. Her anger hits a fever pitch in "Performance Review," when Dwight asks a question as to Michael's "boning Jan," which confirms for her that rumors have officially gotten out of control. It is also the first time we see Jan's tendency to turn to something unhealthy when she becomes angry, as she storms out into the parking lot and begins smoking when her temper reaches a boiling point. Her tendency to turn to her vices as a response to frustration is a bit of foreshadowing that we will see again as the series progresses.

As Season 2 progresses, Jan appears to have developed an intense dislike for Michael, which culminates in the episode "Boys and Girls," where Jan comes into town to do a "women in the workplace" seminar, which Michael is extremely jealous and disappointed that he is not invited to attend. When her anger at Michael again boils, she throws him out of the meeting and publicly emasculates him in front of the rest of the women. Her tendency to emasculate Michael is again a theme that will continue throughout the series, as evidenced in the episode "Women's Appreciation," where Michael reveals that Jan makes him dress up like a schoolgirl, and also makes tapes of their sexual encounters and gives them to her therapist for them to critique. He also reveals that Jan refuses to stop having sex when he wants to, despite the fact that he repeatedly uses their safe word.

All of the problems that have been developing over the course of Season 2 come to a head during the episode "Valentine's Day," where Michael reveals to all of the other branch managers that Jan is his girlfriend, which creates a serious corporate issue that potentially places both Jan as well as Michael's job in jeopardy. Much like in the episode "The Client," Michael again finds a way to salvage the situation, and once again Jan passionately kisses him, repeating the cycle of loathing and attraction that has been established in earlier episodes.

Jan's struggles continue from that point, but she is able to get control of herself and firmly reestablish herself as an authority figure as well as Michael's boss over the next several episodes. During this period, Michael gets a new girlfriend Carol, and leverages this relationship to try and make Jan jealous. As is his custom however, Michael sabotages this relationship, and we cryptically see him inviting someone to go to Sandals Jamaica with him when he is left with an extra ticket.

We find out that person was indeed Jan in the episode "Back from Vacation," where, despite Jan's insistence that they keep their relationship quiet, he again manages to inform everyone about their tryst by sending a racy picture of her to the entire company. It is in this episode where we first are given access to Jan's motivations regarding her relationship with Michael, as well as some other issues in her recent past that have created a great deal of stress for her and continued to influence her increasingly strange behavior.

We find for instance that she has been a victim of identity theft, has begun seeing a psychiatrist, and that her divorce was in part caused by her husband's refusal to have sex with her. This is perhaps consistent with Jan's earlier revelation in "The Client," where we are told that her divorce was also in part because she wanted to have kids and her husband did not. Perhaps we are now finally seeing some of the roots of Jan's decomposition. Her dreams of being a mother are fading, she is getting older and feeling less attractive, and frankly, she is beginning to crack.

She confirms this for the audience when she tells Michael her psychiatrist has found she has some "self-destructive tendencies," which she is told she should actually indulge. She explains to Michael that being with him would mean "lowering her expectations" and that he is "wrong for her, in every way," which he still takes as some kind of compliment. Here we see that Jan has now fully acknowledged (with the help of her psychiatrist), that she has instincts towards behavior that is completely contrary to her own self-interest. We see this idea demonstrated yet again, when she kisses Michael again, and is then repulsed by his Jerry McGuire-like statement "you complete me."

The episode "Cocktails" marks a major turning point for the character of Jan, where she, for the first time, publicly acknowledges having a romantic relationship with Michael, including to her boss David Wallace. Jan's hypersexuality is also revealed in this episode, where she proposes to Michael that they skip the party and have wild sex instead. We also see a theme develop here where Jan seems to be sexually attracted to Michael's idiotic behavior, which is evidenced by her attempting to pull him into the bathroom to have sex after he embarrasses her in front of her boss.

We also hear Jan later reveal that the relationship may have only been appealing to her when it was a secret, perhaps further explaining her propensity for high-risk behavior and difficulties with intimacy, which Michael so strongly craves, as evidenced by his statement, "I want the white picket fence." Her initial speech at David Wallace's house highlights her differences with Michael, as she admits that a best case scenario would include intimacy and normalcy, and a worst case would involve "collapsing into herself like a dying star."

In "Women's Appreciation," we see that Michael's need for intimacy is simply not being met by Jan, who subjects him to a number of increasingly uncomfortable sexual situations. It is in this episode where he first breaks up with Jan due to her continuing odd and aggressive behavior.

The break-up is short-lived however, as Jan ups the ante by getting breast implants, which she uses to seduce Michael back into the relationship. In the final episode of Season 3, we also see that Jan's dramatic mood swings and highly irresponsible behavior have had a negative impact on her job performance, and that she is being fired for this significant decline in her work performance. This puts Michael in a very awkward position, as he is applying for her job at corporate at the same time she finds out she is being fired. Michael is then removed for consideration for the corporate position, and they begin a very long ride back to Scranton together.

It is during this ride that we finally bear witness to the beginning of Jan's complete unraveling. Michael, sensing her despair, invites her to move in with him, which the now completely resigned Jan quickly agrees to. The once confident and assertive career woman now expresses a desire to make being with Michael a "full-time job." She goes on to describe this potential new Jan as a frumpy housewife who completely lets herself go.

Several episodes into the next season, we see that the domestic situation between the two of them is indeed far from ideal, as Michael reveals they are having huge money problems since their cohabitation. It is revealed that Michael has sold his beloved Sebring to help purchase Jan a Porsche, and that he is also working a second job to help keep Jan in the style she is accustomed to. Despite these hardships, we see a Tammy Wynette-like Jan standing by her destitute man, despite the fact that she is nearly the sole cause of Michael's financial problems.

We find out that Jan has big plans financially however, as she is suing Dunder-Mifflin for millions of dollars in a wrongful termination suit, which is documented in the episode "The Deposition." It is in this episode we see Jan's selfish and greedier side, as she steals Michael's diary and uses it to make him look stupid in support of furthering her case. On the drive home we see that Michael's testimony has in fact ruined her case, and that their relationship will be again subjected to further strain.

All of this tension comes to a head in the episode "Dinner Party," where we see how Michael is actually living in his relationship with Jan. In a tour of their home, we see nearly all of Michael's possessions have been removed from the house, and that Jan has almost completely taken over. We see that he is not even allowed to sleep in his own bed, instead being relegated to the foot of the bed, where he lays like a family pet while Jan has the bed to herself. We also learn Jan has started a candle business, and how she plans to us Michael to secure investors for her fledgling company.

We are also introduced to the idea in this episode that Jan likely had an affair with Hunter, her young assistant in New York. This is highlighted by the fact that she continues to play his CD over and over again at the dinner party, which contains lyrics that likely contain the details of their affair, as evidenced by

"You took me by the hand

Made me a man

That one night (one night)

You made everything all right

That one night (one night)

You made everything all right

So raw, so right, all night, all right, oh yeah"

The whole evening eventually spirals completely out of control, as Jan destroys Michael's prized possession, his 200 dollar plasma TV. Eventually the police come to the home, and Michael is advised by the officers that it is best that he leave the house. This signifies the break-up between the two of them, and Michael goes to stay with Dwight at Schrute Farms until Jan finally leaves his home six weeks later.

Although this marks the official end of the relationship between Jan and Michael, we are given a short epilogue as to how her story ends, when Kevin discovers she is pregnant at the end of Season 4, which he immediately calls Michael and tells him. Although Michael assumes it is his, Jan assures him that she was inseminated, and that she might have given Michael a chance if she was younger, but that she has to "make this one count" given her age. She does invite him to attend her Lamaze classes with her, which he eventually accepts after some serious soul-searching.

In typical Jan fashion, she has the baby by herself without telling Michael, which temporarily upsets him, although he quickly rebounds to throw her a baby shower. Here we see glimpses of how far Jan has gone off the deep end, as she sings a lengthy and sultry version of "Son of a Preacher Man" to baby Ass-turd (Michael's interpretation of Astrid), and we are finally given a picture of woman who is completely transformed from the woman we met in the first episodes.

In formulating a DSM diagnosis for Jan, we therefore have to consider her severe mood swings, her hypersexuality, her problems with anger, and her lack of impulse control.

Diagnostic Impressions-Jan Levenson

Axis I- 29.42 Bipolar 1 Disorder, Moderate, Most Recent

Episode Manic

Axis II- Borderline Features Noted

Axis III- None noted

Axis IV- Economic problems, employment problems,

problems with primary support group.

Axis V- GAF 55 Last Year 60

Angela Noelle Martin

Angela Noelle Martin serves as a senior accountant for the Dunder Mifflin branch. Paychecks aren't the only thing she's cutting, as she seems to be judgmental moral authority doling out snide comments to anyone doing anything she believes to be inappropriate. Her personality is perhaps as rigid as it is cold. Her space is overly neat and her attire is conservative which both help present her as the uptight character she truly is.

This all begs the question "why is Angela the way she is?" We must assume something in her life has prepared her for the anal retentiveness and attention to detail needed to thrive in accounting. The only difference between her and most accountants is that most of them know how to "turn it off" and have fun. Angela seems disgusted by anything resembling fun. In an episode entitled "The Fire," all of the employees gather outside as a fire accidentally started by Ryan is extinguished. They decide to play a game in which each employee is asked what three books they would take with them if they were to be stuck on an island. Angela remarks that she would take the *Bible, A Purpose Driven Life,* and the *Da Vinci Code.* She indicated that she would "burn" the Dan Brown novel because, "I hate being titillated." Well as Shakespeare said, "beware of thou doth protest too much."

In psychological terms, being overly moral or "protesting" against certain ills could be a primitive defense mechanism wherein the individual actually finds pleasure in the certain activity. We see this today in many politicians calling up arms to preserve our moral turpitude and traditional family values, all the while soliciting prostitutes, cheating on their wives, or having much interest in graphic and vulgar sexual practices. Is it a surprise that in season seven Angela starts dating a state senator? Most certainly not.

In order to understand her rigid life style and difficulties with people we must look to her earliest of years. We are given bits and pieces of information about her childhood and left to fill in the gaps ourselves. Perhaps the most interesting tidbit is Angela's involvement with beauty pageants, and as a child she was involved in a number of them. But what does this really do to child's delicate psyche? Simply put it gives it a skewed lens to pursue and view the rest of life through. Most children need structure, consistent feedback, support, and a level of creative freedom to learn how to solve problems with their own resolve. We can see how a beauty contest may highlight values that are not healthy. A young girl should not be overly concerned with her beauty; it should be enough of a challenge to get young children washed daily. While parents, teachers, and coaches should be there to give support and feedback, the child is not on a stage to be judged. As is the case with any contest, there can be all but one winner. Being judged on beauty has little to do with things a young girl can have control over, and more to do with politics, luck, and genetics. Children are like sponges; they soak everything up, but unfortunately they have poor tools to interpret their experiences. A child like Angela could be left to come to several rigid and false condusions about life. For example, I am only loved as long as I am winning, or life is a contest where people are constantly judging you, so it's not about fun. Angela, at least in one episode revealed that she enjoys "being judged." Although she sees all others as judges, she knows that she is the harshest judge of them all.

As is common, especially with women in competitive activities involving body image, shape, and performance we see a higher prevalence for eating and body image disorders. Not to say they do not occur in men, but most would agree the pressure that women face from outside sources may be more than their male counterparts. In many episodes we witness her scrupulous eating habits. Many of which involve seeking diets low in proteins and sugars in favor of vegetarian platters.

No matter the conclusion you draw from her eating habits, you see that there is a terrible value she inherited from years of subtle beauty pageant abuse – the fight to preserve youth even at the expense of maturity. In the "Baby Shower" episode, we see Angela cling to Jan's test tube baby, Astrid. Why does she do this? We find out when we see her hovering above a baby swaddled in leafy lettuce snapping pictures with her high resolution camera. We shouldn't be surprised; we've been shown multiple Anne Geddes posters, calendars, and planners at Angela's desk. Her obsession with infantile youth must represent a longing for her own innocence. We understand this to be a metaphor for trying to relive a pleasant time in her own life, a time before pageants.

Throughout her childhood and early adulthood years Angela has come to value control. Likely something that was never given to her as a child, we see her overcompensate for helplessness in early life by her dictatorship in the party planning committee. Phyllis and Angela duel more than a few times of creative control of the party events. No matter Phyllis's logic or tact with Angela, control is not relinquished until Phyllis learns of Angela's infidelity. Angela's over-controlling leadership comes to a head in the "Benihana Christmas" episode. Pam and Karen get so outraged by Angela's lack of cooperation they start their own Christmas party. Angela, fueled by the sudden popularity of Karen and Pam's party, steals their karaoke cord, rendering the main attraction of their party useless. This sort of "win at all cost" mindset has likely come from the pressure to win and the low feelings of self-worth associated with losing beauty pageants.

Not surprisingly, it is easy to see how Angela's childhood development, her perfectionist and controlling tendencies, along with her overall cold and frigid personality all make her terrible with people. She tends to avoid most conversation and interaction with people unless it is absolutely necessary. Unfortunately all people experience a need to belong or be with other people. Much of Angela's needs are fulfilled by her household full of cats and her love of dolls. Her lack of social skills makes interaction with non-living and non-human creatures an easy escape for her. Perhaps the best example of her cold and unfriendly demeanor is evidenced in the "Product Recall" episode. After several reams of paper leave the warehouse with inappropriate water marks, each of the office members are asked to step up and provide their hundreds of customers with support. Kelly, the motor-mouthed customer service specialists, attempts to train Angela and some of the others in dealing with customer complaints. Despite her tutelage, Kelly is unable to get Angela to have empathy for the customers, offering a statement that Dunder Mifflin's official position is "apologetic" but refusing to actually apologize herself for the actions.

In the end, we are left to consider Angela's involvement in the party planning committee to be about more than control, it too serves as a safe refuge for her social interactions. If she can control the settings and details of the interactions of each person in the office, via parties, perhaps she too can set the stage for easier personal engagement. Some social scenes are not always easy for Angela, but those that are prim and proper give her two things – a place to be judged positively and a familiar format to interact with others. People with avoidant personality features often want to be in the presence of others and have appropriate relationships; they just find themselves devoid of the tools necessary to do so.

In order to better understand Angela, we must also understand specifically her closest relationships. No episode shows her disdain of her fellow accountants than "Casual Friday." In the episode, Angela seems to be offended by almost everyone's outfit. Specifically, she is disgusted by Oscar wearing sandals, which expose his bare feet. Not only does she tattle to Toby like a nasty fourth grader, we are also given the impression that she may be targeting him due to her homophobia. Even though Oscar is probably the most polite and knowledgeable person in the office, Angela refuses to accept him because he is gay. Perhaps her convictions are influenced by religion, but we are left to wonder what attracts someone to such strict and rigid views in the first place.

Angela may not completely hate everyone in the office, as evidenced by her relationship with Dwight. Although she prohibited announcing their relationship to coworkers, most seemed to know it was going on. Likewise, she would never show Dwight affection in front of others during their relationship. Her love for Dwight baffles even the most seasoned psychotherapists. Maybe, she saw in him the sort of self confidence she wished she had. Nevertheless, their relationship was ended by Dwight euthanizing her ailing cat in the "Fun Run" episode. Shortly after their break-up she was pestered into a relationship with Andy. We are given the impression many times over that she is not sexually attracted to Andy, as supported by her refusal to engage in sexual activity with him. During most of Andy and Angela's relationship she is having sexual intercourse with Dwight while at work. Quite inappropriate by most standards, especially given Angela's hatred for Jim and Pam's public displays of affection (PDA). While it is not completely clear as to why she would engage in sex with Dwight at work, while engaged to Nard Dog, we have to wonder if it is some sort of compensation for the over-controlled life style she has been living or a means to sabotage her soon to be legal partnership with Andy. Whatever the case we see Angela happiest when the two men are fighting over her.

As previously mentioned, Angela seems especially cold to Jim and Pam. When we examine Angela's cognitive psychological structure we can see that her outright animosity for the otherwise happiest couple in the office tells us more about her and less about them. This protest against the PDA must really come from her own sadness over an inability to appropriately attach herself to another human being in a cooperative relationship. Anger is quite possibly the earliest of the emotions, experienced in all animal species. It serves to protect us when we are unable to rationalize solutions. Her outbursts about others likely come from an internalized sense of anger. Perhaps the anger over her lost childhood or the anger at her own faults causes her to perceive others' happiness as a threat to hers. Early in her childhood she learned that there is but one winner, and if others are happy it must mean she is the loser, and a sore one at that.

There is little evidence to suggest Angela's personality structure would be very amendable by traditional psychotherapeutic means. We could see her being a harsh critic to even the most experienced of therapists. It may be safe to assume that she would have to be introduced to a therapist who she idolizes. It could be worthwhile to pursue religion based counseling services as she may see the pastoral counselor as a higher moral authority than she. Many of her personal characteristics and traits are very central to her core identity. They seem to help her perform her work at a high level, while inhibiting her appropriate social relationships. One should approach these with caution.

Diagnostic Impressions-Angela Martin

Axis I-R/0: 302.9 Paraphilia Not Otherwise Specified, 307.1

Anorexia Nervosa

Axis II-301.82 Avoidant Personality Disorder

Axis III-None

Axis IV-Recent death of Sprinkles the cat, recent termination
of two long-term relationships, and a limited social
support network.

Axis V-GAF: 58

Kelly Rajnigandha Kapoor

Kelly Rajnigandha Kapoor serves as the town crier in Scranton, PA. That is to say, if there is something going on or there is some remnant of news, she will inevitably fuel it to the point of gossip. She reminds us of the annoying sorority girl in college, as her superficiality is rivaled by none Where do you put someone with a mouth like a motorbike? In customer service, and Kelly has the phone skills to run the department by herself.

At the beginning of the show's run, Kelly is portrayed as quiet and anything but her garrulous and shallow self. In fact, she is the victim of Michael's ignorance and insensitivity during "Diversity Day" when she is stereotypically portrayed by Michael as a kin to Apu from The Simpsons. "You want some of my googi googi?" Michael asks. Offended by this Kelly slaps Michael across his face and leaves the room in a rage. It was some time after this event that we see her character change, or at least its complexity finally unfolds.

To best understand Kelly and her bubble-gummy, yet complicated character, it's best to start at birth. It's too bad we are only given the tiniest snippets of her childhood from the episodes, blogs, and office viral videos. Let's start with what we do know: She is an Indian-American and likely born in the United States from parents who immigrated to the country near the time of her birth. We can guess this to be true during the Dwali celebration. Her other family members are more aware and traditional in their culture compared to Kelly. So, if she wasn't born in the U.S., something is fueling her addiction to pop culture and her over-assimilation. We also do not hear the stereotypical accent Michael portrays in her voice, also leading us to believe she has lived in the country for several years. Perhaps the most convincing piece of evidence is her lack of knowledge for her own culture and religion. Dwight actually provides us with more knowledge on Indian culture, and perhaps Kelly knows more about Americana.

We also know that she has four sisters, one of which passed away. Does this influence her Perez Hilton –like love of gossip? Perhaps. If she is psychologically the youngest child, it may explain her immature and superficial infatuation with celebrities. She also seems used to having an audience, which can be typical of some youngest children. We see her expect the patience she likely received at home from her coworkers. Usually Toby finds himself lacking an excuse to escape her long-winded stories, most likely because of adjacent desks in the annex. In fact, people seem to find her quite predictable, enough so they are willing to put money on it. No better example of her coworkers' confidence in her prattling can be found than in the "Safety Training" episode. During the episode many of her coworkers spend the afternoon making a series of menial bets to entertain themselves. One of the biggest bets, at least it appears draws the most people in, was an over-under bet for the amount of time it would take Kelly to explain the process of renting movies via Netflix. Kevin clocked her in at two minutes and forty-two seconds. Additionally, there were a series of side bets for the amount of times she would say awesome (12) and the amount of romantic comedies she would mention (6).

Other than being long-winded, we learn a lot about Kelly by watching how she handles her relationships with others, especially her romantic ones. She has an on again off again romance with Ryan Howard that always provides fans of the show with loads of entertainment. In the episode "The Job," Ryan wastes no time in dropping Kelly like a bad habit. He seems to have no connection to her, while she is almost parasitic towards him. We learn via commercials that Kelly spent most of the summer trying to get over the break-up. She hid under her desk and cried for hours on end. Something very typical of a teenage romance.

Shortly into season four she begins to date the warehouse manager Daryl. We are not sure what the nature of their attraction is, as the relationship begins somewhat suddenly, but we can see Daryl does not play into her childish ways. He speaks very frankly to her, and perhaps this perceived power differential is something Kelly secretly likes. She mentions that she finds him "complicated" because he says "exactly what he is thinking."

During their relationship we see more immaturity at its finest. Kelly gets wind that Daryl has beaten Jim in ping pong and starts taunting Pam. While Jim and Daryl are playing ping pong as a means to escape work and entertain themselves, they find Kelly has pitted them in a no holds barred battle. We see her doing makeshift cheers and slandering Pam. Finally, when Pam get sick of the teasing she challenges Kelly to a game. It turns out neither of them can play, but the jeers and subsequent short-lived match serves to showcase her immaturity.

In addition to her immaturity and chatter-boxing, Kelly often seems oblivious to how other people perceive her. In the "Traveling Salesmen" episode Jim and Dwight try to express the level of customer care they can provide their clients with. They demonstrate the hold time for one of the larger branches, then call Kelly and she immediately picks up. After Jim announces himself, she begins to blabber away as if they hadn't seen one another in years. After only a few seconds he snaps his phone shut and disconnects the call. Kelly, just like in her explanation of Netflix, does not seem to get the subtle hints. Most people would think "something's up" when the whole office is crowding around you with cash while you tell a story or at least take the hint when people hang the phone up on you, but not Kelly.

Similarly, she is either blinded by love or simply unaware of her boyfriends' lack of passion and attraction towards her. Daryl refuses to pick Kelly over his daughter (not a bad thing) when she request a date and Ryan hardly acknowledges they have a relationship at all. He seems to keep her around only as a fall back, as he dumps her every time he has an itch to leave Scranton or reinvent himself. She willingly takes him back every time.

During many of their splits, we see Kelly making threats to hurt herself. She is very quick to cry and seemingly experiences a large repertoire of emotions in a matter of seconds If we were to use common terms to describe her behavior we might call her a "drama queen." She has an uncanny ability to exaggerate even the smallest of life's predicaments. Additionally, she also has a tendency to connect with people too quickly. She reads into most interactions with the opposite sex as being advances on her. Take for instance in the "Manager and Salesman" when Andy sends everyone a card, as to make his attraction to Erin less obvious. Kelly, takes the standard greeting card message as a sure sign of Nard Dog's sexual attraction to her. She spends most of the episode in love, only to find out his heart was set on Erin. While this sort of thing is typical of a teenager with a crush, it is not so with an adult. In psychology we call this type of trait histrionic.

Although she reads too much into common communication with coworkers she is also guilty of trying to gain legitimate attention from them by inappropriate means. We see her in the "Subtle Sexuality" video donned in an adult rated skin tight outfit. Likewise, each Halloween we see a different skimpy and risqué number. Kelly goes as far as to try and impress her style upon Pam, the loveable Plain Jane of the office. Despite meaning well, Kelly can't help but let her own internal logic, namely her belief that women can only be valuable as sex objects, spill into her makeover of Pam. She tries to showcase Pam's breasts, and immediately, Creed, the office creepster, comes in for a prolonged stare. Pam feels tremendously uncomfortable as Creed refuses to budge his nose from her bosoms, enough so she ends up changing her shirt.

We also see how Kelly's psychological character also causes some concern for her health. In an attempt to promote health in each of the region branches corporate sponsors a biggest loser contest, where the office that looses the most weight wins extra vacation days and prizes. We might expect Phyllis, Stanley, Daryl, or Kevin to over-do-it and stress their bodies out, but it is Kelly that takes it too far. Her lack of nutrition affects her ability to think and perform the most basic of brain functions. We see her nearly faint several times until the final weigh in. It isn't perfectly clear how much of her extreme weight loss tactics are to help the team or are influenced by issues with her body. Whatever the case we get the eerie suspicion she has done this sort of thing before, maybe because she truly feels too big or maybe for the attention.

No matter the verdict you have on Kelly, she is a very sweet, witty, and emotional character with whom we all fall in love with. Whether it's her explaining the difference between smack talk and trash talk as she breaks out into an Avril Lavigne tune, or her funny story about digesting a tape worm, sold to her by Creed no less, to lose weight, she does it in a manner that is endearing. No matter how shallow she is, her heart runs deep. All of which serve as some predictor for the outcome of treatment, if she were to ever choose to see a psychologist.

While deep character traits are much harder to alter than simply faulty logic because they are ingrained in her, I get the strange feeling a good therapist could at least accomplish the sand paper effect with her. That is to say, you could knock off all the rough edges. A therapist would have to be on top of his or her game to keep up with all the metaphors taking place every moment with her. On a similar note, just as Toby did with Michael, you'd need to find a creative means to get around her defenses. Some people lie, change the subject, or attack their therapists, but people like Kelly do what I call "drown them." She will likely hide anything important or not superficial by talking a lot. She will verbally throw everything at you in a nervous attempt to not be challenged to change Part of what might work with Kelly is providing an expressive yet structured environment for in which for her to receive feedback. You may find it helpful to give her homework to make a short list of what she needs to talk about and rank her topics. Then she is able to select only the most important ones to discuss in therapy. We see that she is good at dance and has an affinity for pop music; my advice would be to help her create depth in an otherwise seemingly shallow world with this type of media.

Diagnostic Impressions-Kelly Kapoor

Axis I-R/O Anorexia Nervosa

Axis II-301.50 Histrionic Personality Disorder

Axis III-None per reports, referral to physician is suggested.

Axis IV-Identity and acculturation stress, familial stress based on her dating a man from another culture and race.

Axis V-GAF: 56

Conclusion

So there you have it. Our opinions about what's going on with our beloved characters from *The Office*. In some cases, such as with Meredith, the diagnoses pretty much speak for themselves. In others, such as with Michael, we had to use our best clinical judgment, and if you disagree with some of our ideas, that is certainly okay. It is again important to stress how much pleasure we have gotten from watching these folks over the years, and all of these analyses can be taken as a kind of weird homage to all of the crazy things that they do.

As of this writing, Michael has just left the office, which represents a major change to the always entertaining dynamic between these people. Time will tell how this may change people. He is after all, the straw that stirs the drink. In some cases the characters we have diagnosed here, including Meredith and Jan, have held Michael almost solely responsible for the problems in their life, i.e. Meredith's proclamation to him, "you are the reason I drink." Perhaps some positive changes will occur when he leaves, but frankly, given the deeply entrenched patterns of behavior, this seems unlikely.

With Michael's departure, we are also faced with the idea that one day the show will have to come to an end. It's a sad thought, as we have come to know these characters as a kind of surrogate family. Much like a family, people eventually move away and do their own thing, and the actors from this show will have to as well. What will remain (in syndication and otherwise) is a wonderful record of some very memorable and often lovably bizarre people interactions.

In closing, thank you for joining us on this journey into the psyches of some of our favorite imaginary people. It is important to stress the imaginary part, because, although we have had a lot of fun laughing about their various afflictions, many of the things they suffer with would be considerably less humorous in real situations. Because they are caricatures, we are able to step back and take a look through a humorous lens, and perhaps even see some of our own silliness in their constant bumbling and stumbling. This is the genius of a show that has personally brought us years of great laughter, and we for one will continue to be glued to the screen every Thursday to see what they do next.

Made in the USA
Middletown, DE
05 March 2018